BL: 4.2
PTS: .5

D1479550

CANCELLED

ANIMALS OF THE CORAL REEF

UNDER THE SEA

Lynn M. Stone

Rourke Publishing LLC
Vero Beach, Florida 32964

www.rourkepublishing.com

PHOTO CREDITS:
All Photographs ©Marty Snyderman

EDITORIAL SERVICES:
Pamela Schroeder

Library of Congress Cataloging-in-Publication Data

Stone, Lynn M.
    Animals of the coral reef / Lynn M. Stone.
        p. cm. — (Under the sea)
    Includes bibliographical references (p.).
    ISBN 1-58952-109-9
        1. Coral reef animals—Juvenile literature. [1. Coral reef animals.]
        I. Title.

QL125 .S76 2001
591.77'89—dc21   2001019426

Printed in the USA

TABLE OF CONTENTS

ANIMALS OF THE CORAL REEF

Some of the most colorful and amazing places on Earth are coral reefs. Coral reefs are rocky undersea shelves with ledges and boulders. They are filled with rough edges, cracks, and holes. They are hiding places for animals from every major group of **marine** animals.

Branches of a sea fan reach from a coral reef.

Coral reefs are the homes for thousands of different kinds of sea animals. A single reef may have more than 3,000 animal **species**! Some animals are so colorful they look painted. Some have weird and wonderful shapes. A few look more like plants than animals.

Rainbow-colored fish live on the reefs along with giant clams, tall sponges, and spiny sea urchins. Crabs, lobsters, and sharp-toothed moray eels live on coral reefs, too. Sharks and sea turtles swim in the reef water above fancy marine worms, **anemones**, and corals.

A graysby swims out of a vase sponge which, like the sea fan, is a simple animal.

CORALS

Coral reefs are named for small, simple animals called corals. Corals have no bones, eyes, or feet. They are related to jellyfish and sea anemones.

Most kinds of corals live in warm, clear seas, like the Caribbean. Hard corals make a rock-hard "cup" of limestone. The cup is the coral's skeleton, even though it is outside the coral's body.

These feeding parts of coral, called polyps, are surrounded by tentacles.

Coral bodies are soft and sack-like. But a coral animal can reach its finger-like **tentacles** beyond its skeleton cup. Corals catch and eat tiny animals that float past their tentacles. Tentacles reach and grab for **prey**, but they can sting, too. Corals also make food with the help of tiny **algae** plants.

Corals that make limestone skeletons are "hard" or "stony" corals. Most hard corals live together in large groups called colonies. Algae helps the skeletons blend into reefs. Living coral live on top of the old skeletons of dead coral.

Fish hide in staghorn coral.

A crown-of-thorns sea star feeds on coral.

This banded moray is opening its mouth to breathe, not bite.

There are hundreds of coral species. Many grow skeletons in the shapes of deer horns, mushrooms, brains, and lettuce!

Most coral reefs are found in the seas around Indonesia, the Philippine Islands, the Pacific Islands, Brazil, the Gulf of Guinea, the east coast of Africa, the Caribbean, the Bahama Islands, and Australia. Australia's Great Barrier Reef is 1,200 miles (1,935 kilometers) long. It is the world's largest coral reef.

The only living coral reefs off the mainland USA are in the Florida Keys.

ANIMALS WITHOUT BONES

Many animals on a coral reef have no bones. They may or may not have a shell. Either way, they have no skeleton inside their bodies. Some of these animals are corals, sponges, sea cucumbers, jellyfish, clams, worms, starfish, sea squirts, sea urchins, and snails. These animals are **invertebrates**. Invertebrates are some of the sea's most interesting animals, like feather duster worms. They look like flowering plants!

16

Through their tentacles, feather duster worms filter water for food.

One family of invertebrates has some of the sea's best-known little animals: sea biscuits, sea urchins, starfish, brittle stars, basket stars, and feather stars. The crown-of-thorns sea star eats corals and can kill living reefs.

Each animal on the reef has to eat to live. An animal may eat other animals, plants, or both plants and animals. Sooner or later, every animal of the reef finds food—or it becomes food for another animal.

Spanish dancer nudibranch, a sea slug, is a snail without a shell.

FISH

Most large animals on a coral reef are fish. Fish can hide and find food on reefs. Most fish on reefs eat smaller animals. Some of the biggest fish on coral reefs are sharks, rays, barracudas, groupers, and moray eels.

The parrotfish has powerful jaws to bite off chunks of coral rock. The fish spits out the rock. It eats the soft coral inside. Butterfly fish nip off the upper part of soft coral bodies.

A parrotfish chews off pieces of coral skeleton to reach the soft animals inside.

Some fish hunt by hiding. Their color blends in with their surroundings. This is called **camouflage**. The trumpetfish can hide easily. It looks like a branch of soft coral! When a smaller fish passes by, it doesn't see the trumpetfish. Then the trumpetfish grabs it.

Many other species of fish live on the reefs. Some, like the clownfish and blue-striped grunt, wear bright colors.

GLOSSARY

algae (AL jee) — a group of rootless, non-flowering plants, many of which are seaweeds and live in salt water

anemone (an EM on ee) — a kind of soft, simple, marine animal with tentacles

camouflage (KAM eh flahj) — the ability of an animal to blend into its surroundings

invertebrate (in VER teh brit) — any one of several groups of boneless and usually small animals, such as spiders, worms, snails, crabs, and starfish

marine (meh REEN) — of the sea

prey (PRAY) — an animal that is hunted by another animal for food

species (SPEE sheez) — within a group of closely related animals, such as sharks, one certain kind (*reef* shark)

tentacles (TEN te kelz) — a group of long, flexible body parts that usually grow around an animal's mouth and are used for touching, grasping, or stinging

INDEX

Further Reading

Burton, Jane and Taylor, Barbara. *Look Closer: Coral Reef*. Dorling Kindersley, 1992

Cooper, J. *Coral Reefs*. Rourke Publishing, 1992

Marquitty, Miranda. *Ocean*. Dorling Kindersley, 1995

Websites To Visit

- www.abfla.com/parks/JohnPennekamp/pennekamp.html
- www.ovi.com

About The Author

Lynn Stone is the author of over 400 children's books. He is a talented natural history photographer as well. Lynn, a former teacher, travels worldwide to photograph wildlife in their natural habitat.